THE CHALLENGES OF CHANGING CAREER

By

Deborah Siegel

Table of Contents

INTRODUCTION—SAME OLD—SAME OLD.......4

CHAPTER ONE - TRANSITIONING TO THE NEW YOU 8

   Improving Your Appearance 14

CHAPTER TWO—ARE YOU PREPARED?..........27

CHAPTER THREE - REALISTIC EXPECTATIONS .35

CHAPTER FOUR—WORKING THROUGH THE "WHAT IFS"...42

CHAPTER FIVE—BATTLING THE LEARNING CURVE 48

CHAPTER SIX—THE FAMOUS TEN 52

CHAPTER SEVEN—THE ONLY CONSTANT IS CHANGE...62

CHAPTER EIGHT—LOOKING FORWARD TO THE FUTURE..67

CHAPTER NINE—MAKING YOURSELF OBSOLETE 71

CONCLUSION—BEING HONEST 75

The challenges of changing career

INTRODUCTION—SAME OLD—SAME OLD

There are many reasons why people make a career change, and they seem to be doing a lot of it lately. In fact, Jeff Neil of the New York City career counselor said, "Based on my experience, I believe the typical person has six to seven careers, and the number is growing." While six or seven total career changes may seem excessive, keep in mind we have recently been through a severe recession where thousands of companies were downsizing or going out of business altogether. These greater number of career changes could be in direct response to the dictates of a poor job market, but that's not really what we're going to be discussing. If you've been considering a career change because you're tired of the same old—same old, read on my friend.

Assuming you've already been tempted to make the change, what we want to help you with is examining all the challenges that may come with that decision. We'll help you to overcome the challenges of your career change so that you are prepared to be highly successful in your new endeavor. Whether this is your first career change, or perhaps you're hoping it will be your last, there's a lot to consider when making the move.

Feeling overwhelmed? Put your worries aside and decide to pursue the challenges with an open mind and a positive spirit. Changing your career doesn't have to be a time of panic and chaos. If you prepare a plan for success and set realistic expectations for accomplishing appropriate goals in your new career, the possibilities are endless. Choose to look at a new career with enthusiasm and excitement, and you're already well on your way to making a smooth transition.

No need to rush. Relax in the knowledge that you are going to make a change, and together let's discover the best direction to get you to your final destination in a new and rewarding career. When you make a hurried decision, chances are great that the decision won't be as lasting or satisfying as one made with careful thought and studied insight. What you will learn in this process of change may be just as or even more valuable than the new career itself.

Plan on some surprises along the way—some good, and others—well, not so much. The key to staying positive and enthusiastic is not dependent on the degree of difficulty in these challenges you are sure to face. No! Rather it is in the way you choose to react to those challenges that will determine the ease in which you make the change. We'll help you welcome the positive surprises and negotiate the negative ones so that, when all's said and done, you'll come out the other side with an "I can do it" attitude.

Striving for a "no regrets" career change may be a bit optimistic, but perhaps a "few regrets" one is attainable. Our hope for you is that after allowing yourself to climb over the initial learning curve, and move up the ladder to leadership, you will look back over your journey with a grateful heart for all those who helped you along the way and embrace the future in your new career with a true sense of fulfillment.

CHAPTER ONE - TRANSITIONING TO THE NEW YOU

Now that you've decided to make the change in careers, you'll first need to take a look at the changes you may need to make in yourself to assure you greater chances for landing a premium position in your new career. Even if you have chosen to go the entrepreneurial route, your new career will probably require you to make many new contacts and expand your list of business associates. Ask yourself, could your appearance place you at a disadvantage when attempting to achieve success in your newly chosen career path? If you cannot answer unequivocally "no" to that question, then it's time to create a new look to accompany your new career.

This new look is not only with your outer appearance, but also with the looks of the self-promotional materials you will be using in your new career. Both your promotional materials and your personal appearance must be an outstanding fit for your new career. Don't misunderstand; this new you may not necessarily mean expensive and fancy. For example, changing careers from corporate to creative may mean exchanging suits for sweats. Either way, you need to appeal to the hiring pool or to clients whom you hope to attract.

One of my business associates, Clarrisa, moved from an executive position with a major real estate firm to owning her own pet grooming salon. It was a huge change that required a total make over in her daily attire. She had become comfortable with her formal appearance, and it was a challenge for her to feel confident in scrubs and tennis shoes. Two years went by before Clarrisa could part with her tailored suits and stilettoes. They hung in her closet like a testimonial to a career that she could return to if she failed to make a success of her new business. Two years and half a million dollars in annual income later, Clarrisa confidently embraced a more casual self. From nose to toes, she transformed herself into a fun-loving, creative business owner and had a blast with all the changes it required. She still enjoys the comments associates from her past make when they see her youthful appearance and more relaxed, happy outlook on life. However, the changes came with some pretty heavy-duty challenges in the beginning.

When Clarrisa left the safety of her corporate position to expressing her desire to become a groomer and own a pet salon, family, friends, and business associates thought she had lost her mind. After the laughter, when they realized she was dead serious, they tried every way imaginable to discourage the career change. She was making a reasonably good salary, worked under managers who were fair and appreciative, but Clarissa wanted more fun, more joy and happiness, more time to stop and smell the roses. So, she fought their negatives and went ahead with her complete and total career change.

Clarissa learned her craft, opened a grooming salon, and is now the proud owner of several successful upper-end pet salons that cater to the rich and famous. Not only did she face the challenges of her career change, but she took the past professional successes she had experienced and incorporated them into her new business. Before opening day in her first salon, Clarissa sent out special invitations to all her previous business associates who were dog owners and invited them to attend a special pre-opening event for them and their four-legged friends. She had food catered from a first class restaurant, and gourmet doggie treats for their pets. From that moment on, Clarissa set the tone of her pet spa as one that addressed the needs of professionals who treated their pedigree pooches to nothing but the best.

Although Clarissa's personal appearance is casual and appropriate for her new career, she made sure the spa was decorated to appeal to her planned clientele. Her front room is decorated much like the lobby of the real estate offices she left behind, with cushiony leather chairs and an over-sized dark wood reception desk. Her receptionist carries herself much like the one in the offices she left as well, with politeness and polish. Obviously, Clarissa is catering to the needs of her professional clients. Their dogs would probably prefer a fire hydrant, chew toys, and a large box of milk bones.

My point is Clarissa had a great plan that allowed her to embrace a new career in a totally different way and welcome its challenges. She didn't give up all the knowledge from her previous career; instead, she incorporated it to make her pet grooming salon outstanding and appealing to her targeted clientele. Clarissa combined all her knowledge and experience into one big package and continued being the professional she had always been, with the exception of being much more satisfied and prosperous. Not a bad trade, huh?

Learning from Clarissa's story, you should be realizing that all you have done in your previous careers can be used to enhance your future career choice. If you were good with people in a previous career, use those same people-pleasing techniques to ensure success in your current career choice. If you did a great job marketing, advertising, and organizing before, you'll be able to use those same skills as you move forward. So, if you spent a good many years building up to the position you're in now, not to worry. You've just been preparing for the career you're about to have. All is not lost!

Improving Your Appearance

Entering your new career can be quite stressful, so it's important to look and feel your best. This usually means a bit of a make-over. If it happens to be a "nose-to-toes" remodel job, face and conquer the challenge before you meet all the other challenges. The more time you have to get comfortable with the new you, the better you'll be able to present that new you to co-workers and clients.

Take an honest evaluation of yourself and try to see you as other people do. When taking a self-inventory, ask yourself these ten important questions:

1. **Is your hairstyle up-to-date and appropriate?** If you're really in need of a major over-haul, there's no time like the present. Give yourself a fresh

new cut, perhaps a little youthful color (even if you're a guy).

2. **If you're a woman, what does your make-up say about you? If you're a man, do you need to re-think the facial hair?** This is usually more difficult if your new career is more of a white collar position. If you're a woman who has avoided wearing any make-up since the beginning of time, you'll be surprised at the sizeable investment that will be needed to replenish your supply of finery. On closer inspection, some of you will see that less is more. It's no longer appropriate to wear eyeliner that stretches to the temple or the vampire red lipstick. If you're a man who takes pride in the outdoorsy, wilderness look and your new career is with a conservative corporation, pull out the razor and say goodbye to the bush.

Most of the time, the changes are not that drastic or apparent, but they'll need to be made all the same. Do your homework. See how others look who are in the industry you're entering. You don't have to think like everybody else, and in most cases that's a good thing. However, you don't want to stand alone because your looks are offensive or odd. Better to belong and let your creative ideas and hard work set you apart from the crowd.

3. **What about your over-all weight?** If you are as thin as a rail and your new career is to be executive chef at the finest eatery in town, pack on a few pounds. Nobody trusts a skinny chef. Or, if you have let yourself balloon out and your newly chosen career is to be a runway model, back away from the table and run to the nearest gym. I tease! Again,

the need to change your appearance is usually not that extreme. You may have to take a closer look at the subtle changes that need to be made, so spend some time with truth. What definitely needs to go? Unfortunately, weight can cause a great deal of prejudice when it comes to changing careers. If you're too thin, people think you are stressed all the time or have ADHD. If you're over-weight, people think you are lazy and won't perform your job well. So, now is the time to make that New Year's resolution, that you have continuously made for the past decade, come true.

4. **<u>How appropriate is your attire</u>?** I hate to be the one to break it to you, but the days of polyester leisure suits and fishnet nylons are definitely out. Again, just kidding. Most of the time, I find

that people who have not updated their wardrobe have a personal relationship with dark, solid fabrics. Don't be afraid to wear color, prints and, if your career allows, some trendy things as well. The best thing to do is, again, look at others in your new career and see what they are wearing.

I once worked for a national speaker, and she wore the most beautiful clothes on her public engagements. In fact, she was known for her expensive suits and beautiful shoes, and that was exactly the problem. She got more emails from people commenting on her good taste and beautiful clothes than she did on her seminar topics. Once an attendee actually said to her, "I came to see you the last time you were in our city. You look even more amazing today than you did the last time." Not one word was mentioned about what had been taught.

If the speaker had been teaching about fashion or design, perhaps that would have been a good thing. However, her seminars were on sales and successful management styles, and that's the message she wanted remembered. She decided to wear more muted colors and tailored suits, and soon her sales methods grew to be more sensational than her suits.

Dress appropriately—whether it's dressing down or up. It could also be dress that fits the region in which your career will be performed. For example, if you're breaking into the corporate world, but the location is in Hawaii—a tropical shirt or sundress would be appropriate.

If your location is in hot, humid weather or at North Pole type temperatures, dress appropriately.

5. **What does your footwear look like?** Shoes have become quite the fashion statement these days—for both men and women. While you want to be stylin', it's also most important to be comfortable. When it comes to footwear, I'll take comfort over looks any day. Or, look for the best of both worlds and find shoes that fit well, are comfortable, and attractive. Some tend to ignore the condition of their shoes. Big mistake! Make sure they are clean and well-polished, as well as in excellent condition. It's common to judge a person's success based on the condition of their shoes.

6. **<u>Are your nails manicured</u>?** You may be like Clarissa and changing from a corporate position to more of a blue collar career, but nails still matter. Clarissa had always kept her nails manicured and polished. Because she regularly had her hands in water, she decided to remove her artificial nails and save the money she was spending on manicures. After all, the dogs didn't care. She soon discovered that her nails broke to the quick and her hands were rough and cracked. She went back to manicures but left off the artificial nails.

Another male friend went from the corporate world to selling and distributing farm pesticides and equipment. For the longest time he just couldn't figure out why his sales were in the tank. Finally a caring farmer told him that everybody in the area thought he didn't know what he was talking about because his hands were so soft and his nails were neat and polished. They all figured he was just a know nothing city slicker. His sales jumped dramatically when he roughened his skin and quit getting manicures.

7. **<u>Are your teeth healthy and white</u>?** Very important! I should have asked if you even have teeth. If you are in immediate need of dental work, get that done while you have the time and the insurance in your current career. I've known people who didn't smile because their teeth were in such poor condition. What a shame! If you don't smile, others might mistake you for lacking confidence or being downright unfriendly. Even if funds are limited, many dentists accept credit or take payments. Find

one who does and get the work done. Poor dental health not only looks bad, but it often causes bad breath and related general health problems.

8. **<u>Do you look and feel rested</u>?** You would be amazed at the difference in your appearance when you are getting a good night's sleep. The dark circles under your eyes disappear, and your skin isn't the color of a beluga whale. I think you would agree with me, the gray pasty look is definitely out. Not only do you look better, but when you're rested your attitude is better as well. You aren't wearing that perpetual scowl or squinty eyed look due to lack of sleep. Your hair is also shinier and healthier when you're not tossing in bed all night. I know it can be difficult to get good sleep when you're worried about all the challenges

you face with your new career change, so do something to work off the stress. And, this brings us to the next point.

9. **<u>Are you getting enough exercise</u>?** Not only will exercise help you to maintain the right weight, but it will also assist you in letting go of some of that stress that's keeping you up at night. Exercising with friends or at a facility can also be a great way to network your new career.

10. **<u>Lastly, do you look and act happy and excited about life</u>?** If not, it could be you have made the wrong choice in a new career. Granted, you will have to deal with many challenges during this change, and some of them will require much from you. However, if all these changes don't get you jazzed, if you are feeling burdened by your

decision, then now may not be the time to make that change. Or, perhaps you've traveled down the wrong career path. That is why it is so important to do this work before you quit your current job or career. Don't let the cat out of the bag by telling your associates about your plan to make a career change until you have done your homework and have a defined direction. In a poor job market, you may even want to secure another position or begin building your new business before making a public announcement that you cannot retract.

Most of all get comfortable with the new you and ready to present yourself with professionalism to your new clients. Make sure you can speak confidently and knowledgeably about your new field. Make your test market the bathroom mirror, and practice, practice, practice.

Look closely at yourself and see just how you will appear to those with whom you will be doing business. Then ask yourself the most important questions of all— **WOULD YOU DO BUSINESS WITH SOMEONE LIKE YOU?**

CHAPTER TWO—ARE YOU PREPARED?

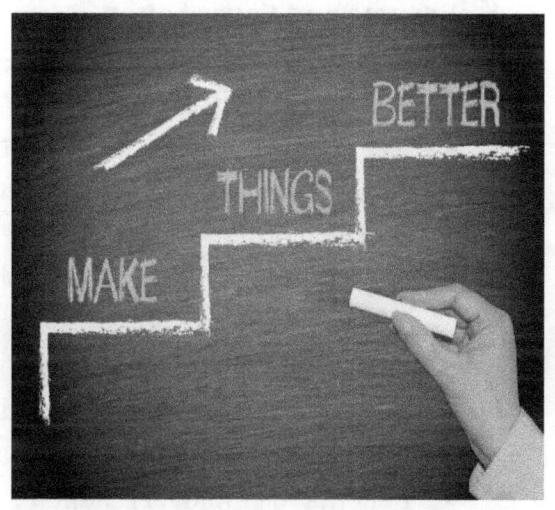

Are you waffling when it comes to that last question? If your answer is anything less than an unequivocal "yes," and you have already done the work on your appearance, here's the next step. Prepare professional looking materials that let your new business associates see you and know you before you've ever been introduced. Let me explain a little further what I mean by professional materials. The following are what I call Five Star Branding:

1. **Resume and Cover Letter**
   - Current contact information—update your old resume
   - List of proficiencies—what makes you excellent/outstanding
   - Special achievements and awards
   - Education and/or experience
   - How you are unique and different from competitors
   - Benefits to employer/clients
   - Hobbies

2. **Professional Photo**
   - Current—not a glamour shot
   - If appropriate, with family, children, pets
   - Not taken with a cell phone—professionally done

3. Business Cards

- Create a slogan and put it on your cards
- Contact information
- Practice KISS (keep it simple stupid)
- Leave white space—don't try to put too much on a business card
- Business or company logo

4. Social Media Presence

- Link or friend influential people in your new career path
- Watch what you put on these sites—it follows you everywhere
- Don't mix personal and professional informational pages

5. Website

- Create a sales page
- Create an affiliates page
- Create a products/services page

- Create a client testimonial page
- Share informational advice from yourself and others
- Link to professional bloggers
- Link to other outstanding professionals in your new career

Once you have introduced yourself through this Five Star Branding system, give the people you will be doing business with in your new career accurate information. Be honest with them, including a non-doctored professional photo. There's nothing worse than expecting one thing and getting another.

I remember when I was going to Arizona State University; I was required to purchase and read one of my professor's books before attending the first day of class. After reading his book, I was stoked to learn from him, excited to meet a professor who was teaching to today's needs. How disappointed I was when I saw him and heard his first lecture. The photo of himself on the jacket of his book was one that had probably been taken a decade ago. His lecture was flat and disconnected; somewhat different than the image he had created in his book. Almost a third of the students dropped out of his class within the first two weeks.

If you are not honest with your branding, you'll have potential clients and employers dropping out before they have a chance to see what you can do. Show them what you're capable of in your materials before they ever meet you. Have your Five Star Branding materials done professionally and honestly.

As well as preparing yourself and your branding materials for the change, you also need to think about how you're going to prepare your family and friends. Doing so will minimize the stress from those who may have reservations about your decision to change careers. The older you get, the more responsibilities you have, the more entrenched you are in your current career, the more preparation it will require for all parties. You will need to prepare them for the changes and challenges, and they will have to prepare themselves to accept your choice.

Think about what this will mean to all involved. Will it mean a temporary financial strain on your family? Will it mean you will have less time to devote to your children and/or spouse? Will this career change mean you will have to deal with envy or jealousy from friends and loved ones? Whatever the challenges, they will need to be prepared right along with you.

There will be some things you cannot foresee, but the challenge will raise its ugly head when you least expect it. This happened to Tracy. Tracy was a highly intelligent, breathtakingly beautiful young lady married to an older, well-established executive. She had worked alongside her husband in their company for several years when she decided she wanted to be an at-home artist. Tracy's husband had always been supportive and encouraging, and there was no reason to think he would have objections to her plan.

For the first year at home, Tracy was attending some art classes to brush up on her skills and hone her artistry. Her husband gradually became more and more crumbly, complaining about everything under the sun. On the brink of divorce, Tracy sat down with her husband to discover his dissatisfaction. She couldn't have been more shocked. Tracy happened to change her career at the time her husband was going through a mid-life crisis that carried a whole other set of challenges for him. He felt abandoned when Tracy left the company to practice her art at home, and worried that she had another man in her life and was seeing him at home while he was at work. The only thing Tracy had done wrong was fail to properly prepare her husband for her career change.

Don't be caught off guard like Tracy. Once you have done your investigative homework and determined some new career choices, share them with your family and talk about what they will mean to the family. You will be amazed at what some of the objections will be, but better to be amazed in the beginning than unprepared in the end.

CHAPTER THREE - REALISTIC EXPECTATIONS

When you are dreaming of taking on a new endeavor, keep in mind you're dreaming. Dreams are not based on facts; they're based on fantasy. At this dream state, that is exactly how you will be looking at your new career choice; it will be a fantasy. Your new career will rarely be as stable as you dreamed of it being, and your financial situation won't either.

Knowing your expectations are somewhat unrealistic in this initial dream state, prepare ahead of time to meet the challenges to come.

No matter how many experts in the industry you interview, take what they say with a grain of salt. If they share what their profits are, decrease those profits by at least 30 percent. There are many reasons why you cannot take as gospel what owners in your chosen industry tell you about the profits of their business. For instance, they may have pumped up the figures to impress you. They may have achieved the numbers they are sharing with you, but what they aren't telling you is how much it cost them to get there. What did they pay out in expenses? What was their payroll? What were their losses? So much goes into the figures provided; they simply cannot be trusted unless you see hard data. Some simply don't know the difference between net and gross.

Next you must be realistic about your time—how much time will it take you to reach an acceptable level of profitability? How many hours will you work in a week's time to make sure your numbers are where they should be? How much are you willing to sacrifice? Let's face it, if it were so easy to make a career change, to start your own business or work your way to the top of your employer's company, everybody would be making a career change. Give yourself time to achieve your goals, and ask your family and friends for their support while you are wrestling with all the challenges of change.

Setbacks are bound to happen, and the only thing to do is analyze what it will take to overcome the latest one and start immediately to hurdle that challenge and move on to the next. Some of these challenges could be as simple as needing additional skills or education, while others require a complete reorganization and change in company culture.

I once heard a story of a gentleman who made a change and took over a company that was poorly managed and inefficiently operated. Managers were overbearing and under qualified, and workers were incompetent or unappreciated. After a month of attempting to bandage the life-threatening wound of a sick company, the new owner did something totally unorthodox. He included a pink slip in every employee's payroll envelope. They were told that they were all fired as of that Friday, with no notice and no severance. Those who wished to return to the company could come back the following Monday and apply for any position in the company they felt qualified to hold. All applications would be considered, including those he had been collecting for the past month from outside hopefuls. The employees would be given no special consideration for time worked because, for the most part, the majority of the workers had been doing just that—simply putting in time.

The company was shut down for several weeks, but the production increased so drastically that the profits gained far outweighed those diverted during the shutdown. Over 80 percent of the workforce returned and achieved greater production numbers than ever before. The 20 percent newly hired were eager and enthusiastic, and their positive energy only served to spur production even more. By preparing for and facing that challenge in his new career, the owner had refused to compromise. By meeting his challenges straight on his strong resolve and outstanding leadership caused the courage and enthusiasm of every worker to grow as well. He prepared them for an opportunity to climb the ladder of success if they so desired, instead of being stuck in a go-no-where position and eventually leaving the company. There's a lot to be said for everybody experiencing a fresh new start, including the owner.

You are probably thinking it was a huge mistake for the owner to have taken over this company in the first place, right? Well, maybe not. We don't know how much he paid for the company, but my bet is that it was only pennies on the dollar for what it could have gone for with maximum production. Perhaps he actually did make a mistake, a huge mistake, but mistakes can be blessings in disguise. Fortunately, we don't always know what tomorrow will bring; if we knew, I suspect we would all want to stay home and hide under the covers.

If one of your challenges is that you realize too late your expectations were on the other side of ridiculous, back up and regroup. That's one thing about changing your career; others' expectations are often on the low side while your expectations are on the high. Your grievous mistakes may be barely noticed by one of your associates. Nobody expects excellence from a newbie, but what they do expect and should get is immediate communication when something runs amuck.

If you know your superior or co-workers are expecting something that you may not be able to deliver, prepare them ahead of time. Solicit their support for a great chance at success. Set a more realistic expectation on both parts, and encourage participation from everybody. Notice I didn't say support from everybody because that might be voicing another unrealistic expectation. However, you can expect participation from everybody, some better than others, but everybody needs to dig in to help overcome the challenges.

If you are working for a company, you can expect your opinions and ideas to be shunned for a while. After all, you're the new kid on the block. You may need to keep your mouth shut and not just jump right into the middle of all the chaos. Even if you believe you have a better way or a more effective success strategy, your expectations are on speed dial and you're moving too fast. Slow it down and get an inside look before you expect your opinions to be valued and rewarded.

CHAPTER FOUR—WORKING THROUGH THE "WHAT IFS"

When heading for major changes, everybody is tempted to play the "what if" game. What if I can't find a job in my new career choice? What if I'm not successful? What if I can't make the kind of money I'm used to making? What if I simply made a huge mistake? That's what I mean by the "what if" game. Sorry to say, this is a game with no winner. In fact, people who play the "what if" game usually do so because they are being plagued by doubt, fear, and uncertainty. It's important to realize that all change is accompanied by these emotions; it's what you decide to do about it that makes the difference between success and imminent failure.

Let's look at Tom's situation. Tom was a middle-aged, middle manager for a medium sized company. His future with the company wasn't bleak, but not very promising either—just mediocre. He probably could have stayed in his position with the company for the remainder of his working life if he was willing to settle for being only somewhat satisfied. Tom's personal life was great, and his financial situation was stable, and that's what had kept him in his current career for longer than he had planned on staying. He just didn't want to rock the boat in his world since there was such a beautiful balance in the rest of his life. However, the more Tom stayed in his mediocre career and position, the more everything started to fall apart around him.

Unfortunately, that's what happens when you become disillusioned with your career. Your previously positive attitude begins to transform itself into a more resentful, unhappy version of yourself. You think nobody notices, but don't kid yourself—everybody notices but they don't want to rock their boats either. So, one person tiptoes around another until the entire environment you live in is topsy-turvy. Still you find yourself waiting for the perfect time to make a change because "what if" you leave and it isn't the right time?

Newsflash! There is no perfect time for change. You may have asked yourself so many "what if" questions that you're sick to death of them. Do me a favor and ask one more. "What if you stayed exactly where you are now and everything in your life remained exactly as it is now? That's an important one. Most people play the "what if" game forward, but I'm asking you to think of things in the right now. Keep in mind, as you stay the same, everything and everyone else is ever changing. For instance, you may continue in your mediocre career, but the industry moves forward and you're made obsolete. Or, you may stay where you are and settle for being unhappy and dissatisfied, but your loved ones move on because they're sick of hearing you complain and do nothing about your situation.

So, if you're fond of playing the "what if" game, remember to ask yourself "What if I never changed and this was what I had to look forward to forever?" If that prospect sticks in your craw, believe me it's time. You may simply need a little more preparation in order to feel secure about changing your career. What you need is a safety net. Here's what my friend, Carla, did for her safety net. Although she was an adult with a family of her own, Carla had learned to ask for the support of her parents. Her parents were financially secure and could afford to help her if she ran into trouble. So, each time she felt ready to make a career change, and she made several over the years, Carla would prepare by communicating to her parents that she may need their help if she ran into trouble. Not once in ten years did she ever have to rely on them for any financial contributions, but she was not preoccupied with worry because she knew they would come through in an emergency.

This was not the case with Tom, the gentleman I mentioned earlier. Tom spent years with one foot out the door. Every time he got close to leaving, he would have an acute case of the "what ifs" and change is mind. He waited for the perfect time, but it never came. He prepared his loved ones that he wanted to make a career move, repeating himself over and over until nobody believed him. Someone even told upper-level management at his company, but they too had heard Tom's story before and were skeptical that Tom would truly leave. After all, they had been hearing these rumors for years. All Tom's talk of starting over in another career had served to diminish his chances for upward mobility in his current career.

This, in turn, made him doubly dissatisfied and regretful.

Eventually, Tom's situation became unbearable and there was no escape except to make the move. He had already burned his bridges before he left his current job. There was nothing for Tom to do now besides jump into a new career with very little exploration and research into whether or not this was the choice for him. As it turned out, Tom had set himself up for failure in both careers. He didn't use the tools that could help him make a successful move, and he had ruined his opportunity to return to his former job. He was caught between a rock and a hard place; any decision from there was bound to be the wrong decision. That's why this book is for you, so that you don't put yourself in Tom's position and stay past the point of no return.

CHAPTER FIVE—BATTLING THE LEARNING CURVE

So, okay—you made the decision to change careers, now what? No doubt there will be a learning curve to hurdle. The higher your previous position was with your old career, the higher you will need to climb in order to conquer the learning curve in your new career. It's not that you have suddenly become incompetent or incapable of learning. What has happened is that you got comfortable with being head honcho where you were and now you are in unchartered territory. It's like you took one giant step forward to make the change and are now shoved two huge steps back.

This is more than likely a phenomenon you'll face. No guts—no glory! It's common for spirits to be at an all-time low just after changing careers because so much energy has been consumed to simply make the decision. Now you're faced with hit after hit of changes to battle and you're still exhausted from the inner war that was waged in order to change careers in the first place. This is the time you are at your most vulnerable, when you are most tempted to return to your old, safe workplace where you have an established reputation of excellence. Don't be fooled, things have changed there as well since your absence. Nothing ever remains the same, so suck it up and move into your career with that same confidence and knowing you had as you left your last.

Be kind to yourself! Be patient with yourself as you are climbing that learning curve. It's an uphill battle, with plenty of pitfalls along the way. Don't let pride stop you from asking for help; you're going to need it to reach success. Those who don't ask—don't get. Be encouraged by all the small achievements during your learning curve. In fact, this is the time you'll want to reward yourself frequently in order to keep moving up and over that learning curve. Nobody expects you to know everything in your new career—nobody except you, that is. If you have chosen to be a business owner, learn from other business owners in related industries. If you have chosen to be employed in a new venture, seek the help of those around you. Make sure you get help from co-workers in lateral or higher positions. As an entrepreneur, avoid asking your own employees to show you the ropes; they are looking toward you for leadership. When seeking employment, be careful that you aren't being sabotaged by an underling who was hoping for the position you took.

Those who are senior in the business are your honey pot—your stream of knowledge and wealth of information. Value what they have done and what they can teach you. Seek their wisdom and advice. Recognize and learn from the mistakes of others who have gone before you. The problem is you cannot hear if you're the one talking all the time. So, make up your mind to observe and absorb. Stop planning what you will say next and sit back, listen to, and learn from those who have made it in the new career you have chosen.

CHAPTER SIX—THE FAMOUS TEN

The Famous Ten are the most common mistakes made by those who have already made a career change:

1. **Consumed with the need to return to your old career.** This is really a need to feel comfortable and safe. Some people who don't allow themselves time to get over that learning curve cannot resist the temptation, so they quit before they

have given themselves a fair chance for success. Don't let yourself assume the awkward position of having one foot in the past and one in the present. If you do, you'll rarely find balance in either.

2. **Too uncomfortable to ask questions**. This is a fear-based problem that occurs in a new company. Facing the unknown can be daunting. For most in a position of knowledge, answering questions is welcomed and appreciated. Nobody wants to clean up mistakes made by a person who was too afraid or incompetent to ask first.

3. **Come into new career like a know-it-all.** Those trying to compensate for their lack of knowledge usually do just the opposite by appearing to be a know-it-all. Believe me, few accept this type of behavior and most banish the know-it-all to fend alone outside their circle of knowledge. Humble

yourself, and others will be happy to help. Recognize you have a lot to learn, and show those in power that you want to learn from the best.

4. **Talk negatively about other career, job, and associates**. Be gracious when speaking of your previous career associates. Negative talk only surrounds you with more negative, so whenever they think of you—they think of all the negative you create. Why not make a positive choice and speak well of your prior position, company, and associates?

5. **Align yourself with the wrong people**. Until you know the company culture, avoid aligning yourself with anyone. If it is your own business, don't play favorites. You will be known by the company you keep, so keep company with the cream of the crop—the best in the business. Unfortunately, you won't really know

who those people are until you spend some time in your new career.

6. **Expect too much**. Once people have made their move and changed careers, many believe they will simply start at a level as high as that they left behind. They have spent so much time dreaming about making this change, but dreaming about a new career and actually changing into one are two completely different animals. Most of us dream about what we like to see happen in a perfect world, but the world isn't perfect and neither will you be in your new career. Shoot for the moon, but expect to travel some distance before you get there.

7. **Settle for too little**. Then there's the other side of the coin with those who settle for too little. Do yourself a favor and believe you can be successful. Dress like a winner; talk like a winner; assume everybody already thinks you

are a winner.   Refuse to settle for anything less than excellence.

8. **Need constant approval and reassurance**. This is a very annoying mistake that many novices make during the first few months of change. It's a fine line between asking questions to learn and asking questions to seek approval and be reassured. Approach your new career with self-confidence and high self-esteem.   Ask questions that will provide you with more knowledge not necessarily with praise or approval. Sometimes asking the questions that uncover a weakness or flaw creates an opportunity for everyone to learn. Seek solutions to the problem instead of becoming one.

9. **Unwillingness to make sacrifices**. This may include a sacrifice of time, money, personal comfort, and even recognition and respect. Most of the time it's a tradeoff. What are you

willing to give up to arrive at where you want to go? Determine and weigh the costs of change before you go all in. It's so much more difficult to handle all the challenges of a changed career if you are blindsided by a loss or are forced to sacrifice something you thought was out of the question.

My husband and I returned to college at the same time—an unfortunate decision that created much unnecessary stress on both our parts. It was my third year in college, and I was worn out from working a full-time job, attending university with maximum credits taken, and being mom to a pre-teen. About this time, my husband informed me he was planning to finish his degree and change careers as well. We did our homework, and planned ahead, and by the following year we felt comfortable enough to assume the additional financial and emotional stress this would put on our family.

Just to be sure we were prepared, we decided to sit down with a counselor and explore our options. I remember the counselor asking us what we were willing to sacrifice. I quickly replied that we had already sacrificed greatly, and we knew what sacrifice was all about. Again the counselor asked what we were willing to sacrifice. Every time she addressed another sacrifice, my answer was always— yeah, we would sacrifice that or that. Finally it came to the house. "Are you willing to give up your home?" That one got me! I wasn't willing to give up my home, and I said so. That was not a consideration because the way we had everything figured out, we wouldn't have to sacrifice our home. I left the meeting that day feeling as though we were ready for my husband to go back to school. All was well! All was well until we had to give up our home in order for him to complete his education.

For a long time I resented the fact that I hadn't paid attention, hadn't planned on making the maximum sacrifice. Of course, now that we have years under our belt and a new home that I love, the sacrifice was well worth it. However, I sure didn't believe so at the time. When you think of all you may have to give up, imagine sacrificing the unimaginable. If you can say yes to that one, you're home free.

10. **<u>Fear of making mistakes</u>.** Fear is the great inhibitor for people who are trying to put their best foot forward in a new career, surrounded by new co-workers. If you're the boss, you don't want to look stupid in front of your employees so you let the fear of failure keep you from experiencing the joys of success. If you are working for another, your knowledge and insight may be limited—so, why take the chance, right? People react to fear quite differently. Some talk too much

out of nervousness; some don't talk at all. Some rush through work in fear they will not finish, resulting in substandard quality. Others are paralyzed by fear and accomplish far less than they would otherwise be capable of doing. No matter how you react to fear, a fearful person's creativity and production will be negatively impacted.

How do you stop being afraid? Where do you find the courage? In learning more about your new career—more knowledge means less fear. Knowledge is important, but what you do with that knowledge is what makes the difference between success and failure. Research, study, learn from the masters (both good and bad), and work through your fear.

When challenges pile up and seem almost insurmountable, take a few moments to dream again. One thing about dreaming is that it puts you in a positive state of mind. Dream about what the future will be like in your new career. Dream about being the recognized expert in your field. Dream about having more time to dream. Whatever you do, avoid creating the same old boring environment that you left behind. If you feel overwhelmed by discouragement and depression, take a dream break.

CHAPTER SEVEN—THE ONLY CONSTANT IS CHANGE

A wise person once told me that the only constant in this world is change. How true is that statement! There will be all sorts of changes as you embark on your new career. There will probably be days where the only thing you can count on is change. One of the things I learned to do is to handle a group of small changes before tackling one huge one. I feel great about my success with all the little ones, and soon I'm ready to take on the monster change. Monster changes bring monster challenges, and too many of those in a day can chew you up and spit you out. Monster change has to be saved for days when you are ready to battle the dragon.

Unfortunately, warriors brave enough to fight the dragon's fire are far and few between, and backup is slim to none. You can always find others to champion your side when your feet are not to the fire, but when the going gets tough the tough can be conspicuously absent. When you're marching forward, proud to call yourself a leader of change, it's a wise practice to turn around and see who's following. Those you thought were following may have embraced change all right—changed their minds and decided to abandon the front line.

As challenging as changing careers can be, and we've certainly covered many of those, there are also great rewards. When the challenges threaten to overtake you, think of those rewards. Look back and see how far you've come and how much you have grown by having the courage to change careers. Perhaps your career has changed, but your desire to achieve greater rewards and satisfactions hasn't. The need to be recognized and appreciated in your new career hasn't changed. The spirit of change is still there, it's just dampened a bit because others may be raining on your parade.

The true about the challenges of change is that some things are simply out of our control. Some challenges in our new career just isn't what we bargained on, and no matter how prepared we thought we were—this one is a shocker—a show stopper. Accept the fact that there will be some things that cannot be controlled, so don't try to control them. If your new career means you must temporarily work longer hours, but that conflicts with your personal life, then you have a decision to make. You cannot ride the fence and neither be a good parent or a good worker.   Challenges we cannot control often require we make difficult choices.

When I am tired, distracted and unable to focus, my tendency is to get the huge challenges done and then I can relax a bit. However, that is not always the best method to experiencing success in your new career. For others to perceive you as competent and knowledgeable in your new career, you'll likely need some successes to shield you from the unbelievers. You'll need a few smaller successes to let you know that you have the courage and skills to tackle the monster. Once you're ready to battle the monster, failure could mean the end of your career.

For this reason, give yourself time to gain some success momentum—some time to conquer existing problems that will get the attention of those at the top. Make yourself outstanding and remarkable, so you can create a reputation of promise and potential leadership.   Your new career move will be all the sweeter for that string of minor achievements. Think about it—a lot of little things can add up to one big jump forward in your new career.

CHAPTER EIGHT—LOOKING FORWARD TO THE FUTURE

Now that you've overcome those first challenges and are on your way to greater heights of success in your newly chosen career, think big! Look forward to what the future holds, and expand your dream. Sure, at first your dream was to find the courage to make the jump, but next you'll be dreaming about how high you can jump in this new position. Can you make it all the way to the top? Sure you can!

By now, many of the prevailing issues that have been bothering co-workers in your new career are beginning to bother you as well. Do you shine or whine? I'm sure all of you said—"I SHINE!" But, do you really? Take a look at your attitude and actions over the past few months. Have you been doing more complaining than conquering? If so, guess what? Without even realizing it, you subconsciously decided to whine not shine. There's one thing about changing careers, if you don't change a bad attitude as well—you'll be fighting that same old battle of depression and dissatisfaction.

How do you stop whining when you aren't aware you are doing it? Well, I'm a believer in the theory that like attracts like, so take an inventory of those who surround you. If they are whining, ask yourself this—are you creating a culture of whiners? After all, whiners are who you are attracting? If it is true that like attracts like, then what does that make you? Some pretty tough questions, but necessary ones to examine if you want to take it to the top in your new career.

In fact, your new career may not be so new anymore. So, how do you feel about the change now? When you look forward to the future, what do you see? Do you picture yourself as an amazing leader in the years to come? Why not? Again, do you shine or whine? You might be thinking, *I really don't do either. I'm not leading, but I'm not a follower either.* That's even worse. There you are, walking that fence of indecision again.

In order to make a difference in your new career and fulfill your dream, it's clear you need to expand your horizons. Think leadership! Career leaders and innovators are constantly on the search for creating changes that keep them in that top position. It's not enough to see changes that need to be made; you've got to think how you can participate in bringing about those changes—how you can make a difference. Perhaps you're more comfortable in a supporting role, but be a player all the same. Get in the game and you'll enjoy the fresh newness you felt when you first found this new opportunity. You'll shine!

CHAPTER NINE—MAKING YOURSELF OBSOLETE

If you are powering a huge machine toward creating a new and exciting career and you believe you're unbeatable, think again. If you're like a locomotive eating up the miles to a better you, I've got some truths to share. There will always be a few little snot-nosed kids in a sports car racing beside you to the finish line. They are creative, explosive thinkers who cannot be ignored. Just look at the technology industry. By the time these kids are out of school, the technology they learned there is obsolete. By necessity, todays wiz-kids have been forced to be independent thinkers, learn faster, work smarter, and innovate more than all other generations combined. If you sit back and get comfortable, the geeks will become gorillas ready to steal your thunder. It may be time to shed that locomotive machine and join today's modern racers.

That's what I meant by making yourself obsolete. Be willing to innovate and change your career for the better. Waiting for trend changes only means you're behind the pack, and you're letting others make your methods and strategies obsolete. YOU be the one to make yourself obsolete. Yesterday's new careers are today's old habits.

I remember the last new electric typewriter I bought. I was so proud and couldn't wait to get my fingers on the keys and create. Everything about it was familiar, except it was wonderfully new.

It was like keeping company with an old friend full of new stories. I had just two days with that new electric typewriter before my husband came home with this boxy looking computer. It couldn't possibly do all the things he promised. If what he said was true, what would happen to the company who invented whiteout and ribbon ink? My guess is that they'd become obsolete.

My husband was patient with my refusal to use the computer for about two days, and then he did something I thought I'd never forgive. He hid my brand new electric typewriter—my sleek, light, electric typewriter. What would I do? I had lessons to plan and no quick and easy electric typewriter to use that I had just spent all that money purchasing. Obviously, I got over it and embraced the computer, but I put up a pretty good fight. The lessons learned from this experience have stayed with me all these years.

I learned not to give my husband the pleasure of making me obsolete. Like the kids in that sports car, he raced around my beliefs and gloated his victory when I finally agreed to give the computer a try—and admitted to actually liking it. It was awkward at first, and I still miss the click of that electric typewriter at times, but the amount of writing I was able to do with a computer was staggering. Once I got through the learning curve and refused to let myself become obsolete, I dreamed of bigger and better things. Of course, my husband has never stopped encouraging me to use more and more technology. From social media and online marketing, to skype and iPads, I'm loving the challenges of the constant changes in my career—even though I'm not yet ready to give my husband the credit for my adventurous spirit.

CONCLUSION—BEING HONEST

Let's be honest, shall we? The challenges of career changes are not what we dream about. We dream about the new career, and push the challenges to the back burner. Contemplating all the difficulties a new career brings might keep many of us in a less than tolerable station in life. Isn't that worse? Wouldn't it be better to face the challenges to come and prepare to ride the tiger of change? Let's be honest! If I had a magic potion that would create a challenge-free career move for you, you couldn't afford it.

Perhaps that would be for the best because life's lessons are best learned in the doing—not the hearing. University professors have prepared today's graduates to enter the workplace and be excellent problem solvers. They're put into groups, given a problem, and asked to come up with viable solutions within a short period of time. Sure, they are creative and work well together as a team. Trouble is they haven't been taught to recognize a problem, to identify an impending challenge. Given the problem, they sure are successful, though. Perhaps the true test would have been to have them research the company and identify its problem.

Because we are not teaching this skill, we have few identifying skills. We may know there is a problem with our chosen career, but we are unable to identify the underlying issue that is causing our discontent. Without the skills to identify the problem, how can we go about finding the proper solution? Next, we go on a fishing expedition. Perhaps it's the pay? So, we negotiate a raise and for a while that curbs our need to pursue something else. Or, maybe it's a promotion—more prestige and recognition, but that soon proofs to be just another rabbit hole.

What's the issue? We aren't honest with ourselves. To be honest might require that we make a change that could create disharmony in our home. To be honest might mean that we just spent hundreds of thousands of dollars on an education we aren't going to use. To be honest might require us to change our careers when we've spent the majority of our lives building our reputation, knowledge, and skills in a career we don't like. Honesty is a hard task master, a demanding mistress, a hard-hearted friend.

All of the things we have discussed have first meant that we had to get honest with ourselves. The message is paramount, if you desire a new career, you need to get honest with yourself and discover whether you're truly ready for the challenges that change will bring because the challenges will come hot and heavy. You'll be burdened, bludgeoned, and hammered with challenges, but at the end of the day will you say it was worth it? Will you have no regrets? Will you feel rewarded and ready to accept the next challenge?

Be honest now—there is no half-way house for career changes. You either change or you don't. You either overcome the challenges or you don't. There comes a point where truth abides and honesty will no longer hide. Who knows, perhaps getting honest will cause you to stay right where you're at, and that's much better than lying to yourself about being willing to make the sacrifices, isn't it?

This is a time for awareness, for searching self, for looking beyond what dreams are made of and think honestly about whether or not a new path in life is right for you. Don't be discouraged if you decide against it right now, tomorrow may tell a different story. However, if you still long for a new start, a new beginning, and a totally different career—then start today to embrace your future.